Let's Return to Christian Unity

by Kokichi Kurosaki

Let's Return to Christian Unity

Let's Stop Dividing the Church

by Kokichi Kurosaki

The SeedSowers
Christian Books Publishing House

Published by:
The SeedSowers
Christian Books Publishing House
P.O. Box 3368
Auburn, ME 04212-3368
ISBN: 0-940232-45-6
Library of Congress Catalog Card Number: 91-73463

Preface

Very little is known of Kokichi Kurosaki, except that he died in the 1960's.

There is only slightly more known about the original publication of this book. It appears that it was first presented in English in 1954 by Eternal Life Press of Kobe, Japan, under the title, *One Body in Christ*. Later, the book was published by Voice Christian Publishers in California (1968). Their comment in publishing the book was:

"We deem his work to be one of the outstanding books of our day."

This company went out of business, and for a time another publisher kept the book in print.

On several occasions we have been asked to consider republishing this work, but all copies that we saw had no copyright page nor publisher's address, nor did anyone know anything about the author, nor who held publishing rights.

After a letter arrived from Rodney Stevens of Texas explaining that he held rights to the book and would allow it to be republished, we immediately took a serious look at the book. We were sincerely amazed at its contents, and we moved toward immediate publication. The book now appears under the title *Let's Return to Christian Unity,* which is more descriptive of its contents.

We wish to thank Rodney Stevens for allowing us to republish this crucial piece of literature.

—The Publishers

Author's Introduction

This is the English version of a pamphlet written in Japanese and published under the title Hitotsu No Kyokai *(One Church)*. I have tried to anticipate the viewpoint of the English readers, as they may vary in their religious experiences and in their background regarding these subjects.

This book deals with the question of what the Ekklesia of the New Testament was and how the original unity of the Ekklesia, which seems divided into many parts, can be restored. For Europeans and Americans who have been under the divided conditions of the existing system of Christian churches for many centuries, it will be almost impossible to grasp an idea quite different from what they have now. Especially as the European civilization, which has been inherited by the Americans, is dominated by the influence of the Greek and Roman civilizations, their Christianity could not help being strongly influenced by these cultures.

With this historical background, western Christianity, though it has contributed to the expression and practices of Christianity in many ways, still cannot be said to have fully realized what the Bible expected. Under Roman influence Christianity became very institutional, and Greek civilization produced strong theological and philosophical tendencies. The result has been, on the one hand, splendid growth in missionary expansion and theological expressions but, on the other hand, the unfortunate spread of sectarianism and institutionalism.

It has been otherwise with us Orientals; therefore, we may have something to contribute to the understanding of the Body of Christ as a unity. I have tried to consider the problem of the present sectionalism and sectarianism in contrast to the unity of Christians in the first century. This has been done out of the measure of faith revealed to me through the Word of God by the Holy Spirit.

However, this book is the result of my lifelong experience with fellow believers. They are those people who are endeavoring to live in life-union with God and fellow Christians in Body-of-Christ existence. Thus these believers endeavor to practice the Christian faith according to the simple principles of the New Testament. This is life in Christ without institutional organization. The Japanese Christians I have fellowshiped with are not mentioned in this book, because it seems unnecessary to refer to them. But being afraid that readers may conclude that this seemingly fantastic and abstract idea cannot be realized in actual experience as the Body of Christ, I feel it necessary to add that it can be, for it has been experienced for many years in Japan.

May God bless this work and use it for furthering the spiritual unity of the Body of Christ!

Kokichi Kurosaki
Kobe, Japan

1
Our Present Dilemma

Europeans and Americans have been under the divided conditions of the existing system of Christian churches for many centuries, and they find it hard to imagine anything else. Our background in the Orient has been different, and our different perspective has perhaps made it easier to understand the family relationship God intended for us to share with each other. What I shall say is written out of the measure of faith revealed to me through the Scriptures by the Spirit of God. However, it is not merely the product of speculation, but the result of my life-long experience with fellow believers. Far from being purely theory or speculation, this seemingly fantastic and abstract idea *can* be realized in experience as it has been for many years in Japan.

Divisions Among Christians

There are many foreign missionaries today in Japan who have come from different churches and groups as well as from different countries. The number of sects seems countless to the average Japanese, for there are over a hundred so-called "Christian" groups, each having its own unique doctrine or organization by which they distinguish and separate themselves from others. Though some of them are quite tolerant and willing to cooperate with others, some are very intolerant.

Naturally, the Japanese people as a whole are amazed and often disgusted by the divisions and squabblings of those who profess to know the love of God. This cannot be passed off simply as the Japanese ignorance of the church, for many Japanese have found from reading the Bible itself that this condition is contrary to the fundamental teaching of the Word of God.

The *Ekklesia* (translated *Church* in the English editions of the Holy Scriptures) is the Body of Christ.[1]

As Head, Christ governs, commands and directs this Ekklesia/assembly—His Body, composed as it is of many members with different gifts or functions. Each member is connected to the Head directly, and thus all members enjoy fellowship with each other through their relationship to Him.

Just as faith in Christ is the reality of a new spiritual life in Him, so His Body is a spiritual organism made up of all believers. The construction of the human body and its members is very similar to the essential nature of the Ekklesia of Christ. Indeed, the Body of Christ, though not physical, is not less real and practical than our human bodies. Thus, the Ekklesia has *real* existence, and is *one*

---

[1]Ephesians 1:22,23; 4:15,16; 5:23-27, 32; Col. 1:18; 2:19

Body, and for no reason should it be divided. As a human body cannot live when it is divided into parts, so the Body of Christ cannot live when it is sectionalized. A divided Church is no Church at all in the New Testament sense.

Yet today, to our deep grief, the Church is divided into many hundreds of sects. Though most of them do not openly dare to boast themselves to be the only true Ekklesia, still each of them acts as if it were the only Body of Christ. Having lost sight of the true nature of the Ekklesia, the present-day church is divided in spirit. This tends to dissipate the strength of the Ekklesia in fruitless activity and worldly display. *And still more to be feared is the fact that the church does not realize this dangerous condition; consequently, division after division continues without end.*

The serious practical consequences of this division are very obvious. Innumerable sects from the United States have been sending missionaries to convert the Japanese to their particular sect, even pulling members out of other churches into their own group.

The Japanese are at a loss to know which sect is right in its claim to represent real Christianity. Those who are already Christians are often shaken in faith and hindered in their spiritual growth. Some are led into serious confusion by missionaries, each insisting that *all* Christians who do not hold *their* particular doctrines are in error.

In Corinth, contentions broke out among the Christians, who were saying either, "I am in Paul's group," "I

3

am in Apollo's," "I am of Peter," or "I am just a Christian." Paul said they were *carnal* and pleaded that they "speak with one voice and not allow themselves to be split up into parties." He gave the same strong admonition in several other cases, e.g., 1 Cor. 1:10, 16; 3:5-8; Phil. 1:27, 2:2, 4:2, etc.

Far from being of the same mind and judgment, each denomination and sect has its own banner or trademark.

Though in theory they may accept the idea that others can be right with God (and even, perhaps, a few going on in the things of God), in practice they believe that true Christianity is represented by their sect alone. Seeing themselves superior to others, they attempt to pull all (saved and unsaved) to themselves, and think that only in this way can they be loyal to the Lord.

These sects and denominations, with no qualms over "stealing sheep" from other folds, seem more concerned with converting men to their own group than to Christ. How many of us have tried to convert a brother to this "true faith"? Thus Paul's admonitions are so utterly neglected that the Ekklesia of God is now divided into hundreds of sects and denominations and has fallen into fatal disorder.

What is at the heart of this problem? What is wrong? *All this confusion and disaster is the result of mistaken and false ideas as to the essential nature of the Ekklesia.*

Each sect emphasizes its *peculiarities* as the principal elements of Christian faith, and condemns others who cannot agree. As a result, Christianity is heading down a path of endless division. No one knows what the end will be.

To clear up present confusion and to show how Christians may all live as one in Christ, *it is necessary to rediscover the real center of Christianity.* Let us learn what our Father has made the center of our relationship to Him so that we might make it the center of our faith. Only in this way will the present sin of a divided Christianity be brought to an end.

First, however, it will be helpful to look back and see what has been taken as the center of Christianity in history. In doing so, however, keep in mind that the word "center" is meant to be understood as "the most essential element" of the Christian faith. It might be better to use the word "nucleus" or "essence" or "prime loyalty" instead of "center," but trusting the reader will understand the word "center" as meaning the "essential element," I will employ this word.

2

The Center of Christianity Throughout History

1. The Apostolic Age

To the disciples Christ was *personally* the center of their faith. He lived and walked with them on earth. His unique personality, His noble character, His heavenly dialogues, His daily life full of love, His miraculous power and His authoritative attitude—all this attracted the hearts of the disciples just as a magnet attracts iron.

Believing Him to be the expected Messiah and believing that the promise of God would be fulfilled through Him, they followed Him everywhere as He preached the Gospel of the Kingdom of God. Their hearts and minds were fully satisfied by being with Jesus. Coming to realize that He was not only a great personality but God in human flesh, they worshiped Him—their faith and experience centered in *Christ Himself*.

The death of Jesus temporarily threw the disciples into confusion and darkness, but His resurrection re-

7

stored even stronger conviction to their hearts. Then they began to have intimate fellowship with Him as the risen Lord.

When Jesus ascended to be with the Father, He asked the Father to send His Spirit to indwell them; so then their life was united to that of their risen Lord, and they lived a life of *"koinonia"*—fellowship—with Him and with all fellow believers.

Even in the case of Paul, who had not been with Jesus during His earthly life, this experience of spiritual unity with the risen Lord was most vivid and real, as we can see in his expressions, "To me to live is Christ" and "I am crucified with Christ; nevertheless I live; yet not I, but Christ liveth in me."

The hope of the disciples' Christian lives was the return of Christ, for whom they waited. Their eyes were fixed on the *Lord Himself* as the One who was, and is, and will appear again.

To sum up, the center of the life of faith for the disciples was Jesus Christ Himself *in their spiritual koinonia (fellowship) with Him.* They were baptized in His name, prayed to Him and worked miracles in His name. They found new life in Him personally, and the purifying hope of His return ruled their lives.

---

[2]*Koinonia* (Kolvwvia) from noun plus verb meaning "to share in common" is translated communion, communication and, most often, fellowship. 1 John 1:3 "That which we have seen and heard, we declare to you, <so> that you also may have koinonia—fellowship—with us: and truly our koinonia—fellowship—is with the Father, and with his son, Jesus Christ." (Also verses 6&7)

8

Through the disciples' witness to the risen Christ, many were converted to faith in Him. Being baptized, these converts devoted themselves to the teaching of the apostles, fellowship with one another, to the breaking of bread, and to prayer. Many wonders and signs were done through the apostles. All who believed were together and had all things in common: They sold their possessions and goods and distributed them to all, as any had need. Day by day, attending the temple together and breaking bread in their homes, they partook of food with glad and generous hearts, praising God and having favor with all the people. (Acts 2:24-47)

These were the *practices* of the early Ekklesia, but *none of these practices were the center of their faith.* Their faith was concentrated upon *Christ Himself.* Their living union with Him was the center of their lives and consequently of the Ekklesia.

The apostles did not think of baptism and the Lord's Supper as *sacramental rites.* (See John 4:2; 1 Cor. 1:17; also refer to the Gospels and especially to Luke 22:19, 20 in the RSV.) They practiced baptism and the Lord's Supper as valuable expressions of their faith. But it cannot be said that they made these "acts of fellowship" the center of their faith nor were these the *center* of the Ekklesia.

Neither did the apostles establish any creeds or doctrines. Even the so-called Pauline theology was not theology as understood in its present-day meaning. Theology was only Paul's method of *explaining* faith. It was his expression of his fellowship with God and Christ. It was his witness to his having koinonia with the

9

Lord. Understanding Paul's (or anyone else's) explanation of his faith is one thing, but to have koinonia with the Lord is another.

The former should not be taken for the latter, and certainly should not be made the center of faith. The center of Paul's faith was union with Christ in the Spirit.

The same was true of John. Theological explanation was only their effort to make the central Person more real to other believers.

They were not theologizing, but testifying! In the apostolic age there were some among believers who labored for the Ekklesia, such as the elders and deacons, etc. But these words were only names for those who served the Ekklesia because they were fitted for such ministry. There was nothing like an established institution to *select* them! Their services were naturally recognized as each demonstrated their *charismata,* or gifts of the Spirit...*in* the Ekklesia.

Authority as exercised in the New Testament Ekklesia was not of the legal or institutional kind such as we conceive of today. Like the Lord (cf. Mark 11:28-30), leaders among those early believers possessed *only* heavenly or spiritual authority. This authority was based on their *Spirit-given* ability and was recognized and followed when, and only because, they spoke in the evident power and truth of the Holy Spirit. Even the authority of the apostles was not a legal thing...nor organizational. It existed only by the Spirit's convicting men's hearts. In just the same way, the service of the elders and deacons was completely on a spiritual basis.

If a brother was contentious or determined to go his own way rather than that of the Lord's, they let him go, as did Jesus with the rich young ruler, or Paul with Demas.

Christians in the apostolic age never thought of making an institutional organization part of the Ekklesia, nor of substituting human service or earthly authority for the activity and authority of the Spirit in the midst of their Ekklesia assembly.

2. The Catholic Period

When the Emperor Constantine (313 A.D.) made Christianity a national religion, using it as a means for the spiritual unity of the whole empire, the bloody persecutions of the Roman Emperors ceased at last. After that, Christianity rapidly spread over the whole territory of the Roman Empire.

In this expansion there developed an organization that made itself to be called *"the* Church." This institutionalized system became more and more centralized, until at last a Roman bishop became the "Father" of the whole Roman Church.

European civilization is a combination of Greek, Roman and Hebrew cultures. The Greeks are the source of its philosophical and aesthetic elements, the Romans of its legal and political nature, and the Hebrews of the religious phases of European civilization.

It is true that Christianity in the Roman Empire could not escape being influenced by Roman culture. Imperial

11

authority, deriving its power now from a union of both political and ecclesiastical control could declare all citizens of the state "Christians" and members of this institutional church (which they did). As a result, the true purpose of the Ekklesia (to live in communion and fellowship with Christ and each other as the living expression of His life) was lost within "the Church." This official Catholic Church became just a legal body regulated by clerical law instead of the Spirit. Faith, like the laws of the state, was reduced to a creed, formulated for and remembered by the common members. Those who did not accept the creed, just as those who did not obey the law, were judged as heretics and punished, usually by expulsion or, if necessary, death.

When Christianity was transformed into such a legal institution, it could no more be expected that communion (koinonia) with God and with Christ would be the center of the Ekklesia. The object of faith and loyalty was transferred from *spiritual union* with Christ, as the Head of the Ekklesia, to the legal government of the pope, as the earthly representative of the Kingdom of God. The spiritual Ekklesia was replaced by the earthly Church whose center was the pope as the head. In this Church the fellowship of Christians was no longer the Body of Christ that has life-union with Him; and Christ was no longer the Head who governs His Body, the Ekklesia.

With the establishment of the institutional Church, the worship of God in spirit and truth died out and was replaced by ritual and formal worship.

No more could the words of John be applied to

Christians; that is, that "the anointing (of the Spirit) which you received from Him abides in you, and so you have no need that any one should teach you, as His anointing (i.e. the Spirit) teaches you about everything..." (1 John 2:27). The members of the Church were then being taught only by the appointed officials of the Church.

This was the Roman Church, which insisted that outside her fellowship there could be no salvation. Without the sanction of the pope no one could enter the Kingdom of God. He maintained that he alone kept the keys of heaven. Without taking part in the prescribed rituals and sacraments conducted by the Church's ordained officials, one was not only unable to be a true member of the Church, but was not even considered a Christian.

Not only did the Church teach this, but these principles became the laws of the Church. Those who refused to obey these regulations were ultimately excommunicated, losing as well their legal right as citizens and the protection of the state. To stand against the *institutional* Catholic Church came to be a far more dangerous matter than to stand against the *government* of the state.

Under this coercion men's minds were deprived of the right to freely seek truth and real faith. Those believers who did hunger and thirst after faith and spiritual life had to seek it at the risk of their lives.

Thus, the institutional Church, with the pope as its head, became the center of Christianity. Especially after the system of the Inquisition was established in several countries of Europe, heretics were relentlessly tracked down and cruelly punished by the Church. The Church had become a purely legal and worldly institution whose law had the power of the state.

It was as the result of this policy of Inquisition that Wycliffe of England, John Huss of Prague, Savanarola of Italy and William Tyndale of England were put to death. History bears witness to the tragic consequences of a system that could render such retribution for translating the Scriptures or opposing the pope of Rome.

This severe punishment deeply impressed the uneducated masses. They understood that to reject the authorized doctrine of the Church was the worst sin a man could commit, and that it meant that toleration of such heresy was just as bad. So men were led to think that one's Christian duty was to follow the dogma of the church unquestioningly and to persecute the heretics.

This spirit of intolerance survived even after the Reformation. This spirit exists today in Protestant churches and is the real cause of today's sectarianism.

3. The Protestant Period

In the Reformation, Martin Luther and John Calvin established new churches in several parts of Europe separate from the Roman Church. The Protestant Christians, the Roman pope and the Roman institution lost their position as the *center* of Christianity. What then was to become the *center* for the new churches that arose out of the reformer's work? Something had to fill this vacuum.

14

For Martin Luther, as we can see in his commentary on Galatians, the central element of his faith was union with Christ in *spirit and life*—that is, koinonia with God. But it was the Holy Scripture that led Luther to this faith, and he fought against the Roman Church, using this Book as his sole weapon.

All the other reformers likewise found in the Bible the whole source of truth. In rejecting the authority of the Roman Church, these men turned to the Scriptures as the authority for their faith and actions. *In the fierce conflict of those early days of the Reformation, it was natural that they should seek the security of some objective standard to meet the seemingly unlimited politico-ecclesiastical power of Rome.* Therefore, the position of the *Bible* as the God-inspired testimony of the apostles' personal faith in Christ gradually changed and became the source of Protestant "dogma" and the criterion of acceptable faith. *Replacing the Roman pope, the Bible became the center of the Protestant churches.*

Luther's rediscovery of the great Biblical doctrine of "salvation by faith alone" was one of the greatest events of human history. His restoration of the Bible to its rightful place as the basic source of Christianity was real progress. Compared with the faith of the Roman Church, it was a tremendous step in returning to the original New Testament faith.

However, it was felt necessary in Protestantism, as it had been in Catholicism, to make a clear-cut distinction between orthodox and heretical faith and to exclude heretics from the new, purified church. So there came to be little difference between Protestants and Romanists in this area. Both insisted on making a clear, outward distinction between "real Christians" and heretics.

As a result, the Protestants were forced to spend a great deal of effort formulating creeds. This produced many excellent statements of scriptural truth.

Faith is life in Jesus Christ, and a life can never be confined within certain systems or creeds.

Creeds are not the end of faith; they are *expressions* of our fellowship with Christ. They must not be mistaken for the object or center of our faith. Obviously the fullness of the living Christ cannot be held within the narrow limits of written creeds.

The Bible itself is but the description of this life; it is a description of God in His relationship to men. Consequently, Scripture contains many seeming contradictions arising from the complex and varied nature of the lives of individuals and their experiences with God. This variety will forever prevent us from summing up the truth of the Bible in any fixed creeds or confessions. Creeds can never be more than one person's or one group's understanding of the truth. Creeds are limited in what they can do.

The failure to understand this limitation of creeds has given rise to unavoidable disturbances in Protestantism and has become the cause of the division of Christendom into many sects and denominations. Division has happened because of different interpretations and understandings of teachings in the Bible.

The first famous dispute among Protestants broke out

16

between Luther and Zwingli over the meaning of the Lord's Supper. In the year 1529, Philip of Hesse, trying to unify the warring sides of Protestantism, brought about a conference in Marburg, hoping to get Luther and Zwingli to agree on certain principal doctrines.

At the conference they could agree on all doctrines except whether the bread and wine in the Lord's Supper were *actually* the flesh and blood of Jesus, or only *represented* them. Because the two men could not agree on this point they would not shake hands, and at last the conference was dissolved in failure, to the disappointment of all. All European and American Christians know the great damage this disagreement has inflicted on the unity of Christians.

A second episode occurred between Calvin and Servetus. They could not agree on the doctrine of the Trinity. Calvin finally caused Servetus to be burned on the hill of Champell. These three best-known Reformation heroes became *examples* of sectarianism. They were naturally followed, or imitated, by their successors, throwing the church into divisions without end. Since this beginning, many hundreds of sects and denominations have appeared in the world, each thinking itself to be the true church, holding all others to be mistaken. This has continued until now, making it almost impossible for believers to be one in Christ.

Paul's admonition to the Corinthians regarding "I am of Paul," "I am of Apollos," "I am of Christ" was *"Is Christ divided? ..."* His admonition is forgotten or ignored, and division is rampant in all Protestant denominations.

17

The points on which the church has been divided will be summarized in the next chapter.

3
Points of Division

Theology

Theological controversy has raged over many issues, the most basic being now the division between an "orthodox" and a "liberal" theology. This has caused great division among Christians, especially when the former falls into dead orthodoxy, rejecting all fresh thought in favor of critical study, and when the latter falls into pure humanism, rejecting the fundamental truths of the Scripture.

These two oppose and fight each other, the orthodox condemning the liberals as faithless, and the liberals despising the orthodox as old-fashioned disregarders of science and worshipers of the letter of the Bible (bibliolatry).

There are many other lesser theological distinctions, creating wide conflicts among Christians. So if you take theology or creed as the center of Christianity, it naturally follows there must inevitably be a division of Christians.

Inspiration of the Scriptures

One might think that with the Bible as the center of Christianity, the unity of Christians could be easily realized. Unfortunately, this has not proved to be true. This inability of Scripture to unify the Lord's people proves that the *letter* of the Bible cannot really replace the living Christ as the center of our faith.

The Bible speaks to us of the life and work of God, and since "life" is greater than its manifestation, it cannot be expressed completely in any logical or theological form. Therefore, the Bible itself cannot escape being understood in many different ways. Thus we see how, in the wisdom of God, it is impossible to make the Scriptures the end or final authority in themselves, for they only express God's authority *to those who live in fellowship with the Spirit*.

On the one hand there are the so-called *fundamentalists* who, accepting the Bible as the "infallible Word of God," believe there is no mistake in the whole Bible, not even in one phrase or manner of wording. To them it is, in the most literal sense, the Word of God from cover to cover, and their faith is utterly dependent on its literal infallibility.

On the other hand there are *liberals* who try to compromise Biblical truth with science. Denying the spiritual in favor of the rational, or adopting the results of higher and lower criticism, they reject the inspiration of the whole Bible.

There are yet others who take the whole Bible to be the Word of God as do the fundamentalists, but in a little different way. They believe that the Spirit acts in the *words* of the historical records to reveal the *Living* Word. They recognize the Bible as the record of God's revelation of Himself throughout history, climaxing in Christ— an inspired record resulting from the activity of the Spirit in the individuals who wrote it.

Part of the problem in approaching the Bible arises from its very nature, i.e., the way in which God saw fit to give it to us. When the rays of the sun pass through a lens, they are diffused according to the quality and shape of the lens.

Just as the study of the quality and shape of a lens is necessary to know the nature of the original rays that passed through it, so to fully understand the will of God through the written record, the circumstances of history in which God revealed Himself and the character of those through whose instrumentality His Word has been transmitted to us must be studied.

Perhaps God allowed these "limitations" of the written record so that *factual* knowledge and *intellectual* understanding of the Bible might not become an end in itself...might *not* be central.

At any rate, we should avail ourselves of such studies and knowledge of the Scripture, and seek, in dependence on the work of the Spirit, *to come into personal relationship with Christ, the Truth Himself.* For apart from *both* the written Word and the quickening Spirit there is little or no real experiential knowledge of Jesus, Who is the living Word of God.

Interpretation of the Scriptures

Many have put great emphasis on certain texts of the Bible and have built up sects upon those few texts, disregarding the context and the general teaching of the whole Bible. For example, the "Holiness" groups tend to overemphasize the doctrine of sanctification and, selecting some verses which seem to teach it, insist that entire and perfect sanctification is attainable in this life. The "Friends," emphasizing the "inner light" and the fellowship of the Spirit, seem to neglect even such important doctrines as redemption through the blood of Christ.

However, in condemning such extremes, we should remember that these groups may have had sufficient reason for their appearance when, because of dead orthodoxy, many Christians became very loose in their moral lives. Believing that Christ was judged on the cross as their substitute, they neglected the practical results that really believing this truth always produces.

Others, though not falling into loose morality, held the dogmas and creeds of Christianity as a kind of diploma from school or college, or as a ticket into the Kingdom of Heaven. Many of these people had no living fellowship with the Lord, yet they saw themselves to be the best kind of Christians. They lacked the Spirit acting within them, orthodox only in their heads and not in their hearts.

Such spiritless conditions among the churches gave rise to those who emphasized holiness and spirituality. *Then, when not accepted by Christians as a whole, they made their doctrine a basis for fellowship within a narrow circle of those who would agree with them.* Thus new sects were born, which in turn tended to disregard other truths and the teaching of the Bible as a whole.

Innumerable sects have arisen in this way. Thus Christ's Body is divided into countless sections. Nothing could be clearer than this: Such doctrinal emphases are a prime cause of sectarianism.

Rituals and Ceremonies

The Baptists separated from other churches because of differences of opinion regarding the form of baptism. Another group was divided over whether they should use an organ in their services— because the Bible nowhere tells us to use an organ. Again, another sect arose over the supposed necessity of women to cover their heads when they prayed (1 Cor. 11:2-6). Seventh Day Adventists insist on keeping the law concerning clean and unclean foods. There are many such cases in which very trifling questions about formal rites have given rise to new sects. In turn, each sect goes about condemning the others, often calling them heretics.

It is very unfortunate for Japan and other "heathen" lands that many of these sects are sending missionaries, making sure this continues in each country.

Conclusion

The Protestant Church is so divided that to realize its unity seems almost hopeless. This has come from mistaking the true focus and center of Christianity and substituting either theology or dogma or creeds or the Bible or institutions or rituals or ceremonies.

Moreover, the divisions were emphasized by the idea, inherited from the Roman Church, that one's own group alone has the orthodox faith. All other groups must be persecuted as being in error. This attitude is now part of the over-all Protestant mind. A great deal of energy is expended by all in refuting the doctrine of other sects and in trying to pull believers out of someone else's sect and into one's own sect.

Where is the unity of the Ekklesia? What has happened to the oneness of the Body of Christ? Why do not we Christians recognize the *sinfulness* of this condition and *repent?*

4

The True Center of Christianity

The Roman Catholic Church, by putting the *institution,* with the pope as its head, at the center of Christianity, had ceased to be an expression of the real Ekklesia. This gave rise to Protestantism, which in turn put the *Bible* in the center, though still largely retaining the *institutionalism* of the Roman Church. This new center also proved *off*-center and has resulted in splitting Christians into many warring, incomplete sects. Thus Protestants, too, have not realized, *in practice,* the true Ekklesia.

Some denominations began to recognize the impotency and wrongness of the existing state of the churches and are endeavoring to remedy the situation by reuniting divided denominations. They seek to form an alliance of all churches into one ecumenical Church. However, this movement is obviously doomed to failure. The very effort to unite the churches seems likely to end only in the formation of yet *another* even *greater* sect.

I say this because the churches involved are *not* re-establishing the true center of Christianity. The ecumenical movement is still caught in the sectarian spirit inherited from Catholicism.

The *Ekklesia* (translated *Church* in the English editions of the Bible) is the Body of Christ, composed of many members. Each member is connected directly to the Head in spiritual life-union and possesses different gifts and functions. This Body is one *spiritual organism*. Being a single, corporate, spiritual entity—*one* Body—the Ekklesia was never intended to be divided. A body simply cannot live and function properly in a divided condition. Yet this is the very condition prevailing today.

What is at the heart of all this? *What is wrong?* Where is the true unity of the one Body of Christ? The answer is simple, yet profound.

The confusion and disaster of sectarianism is the result of mistaken and false ideas as to the center of the Ekklesia. What is the essential nature of the Ekklesia?

The True Center

The center of Christianity is neither institution nor organization. Nor is it even the Bible itself (as the reformers made it). *The Ekklesia existed before the formation of the New Testament canon.*

Christians were in fellowship with God and one another, centering their faith in Christ, long before there was any accepted New Testament.

There is only one center of Christianity, and this center is *spiritual fellowship with God through Christ—life-union with God in Christ.*

When there is this koinonia—fellowship—there is the Body of Christ, the Ekklesia.

Where there is no koinonia with God there is no Ekklesia, because life-union is lacking. Though there may be many excellent clerical personages, many elegant church buildings, many scholarly dogmas and creeds, *if* there is no *koinonia* with God and Christ, there can be no Ekklesia at all. On the other hand, if there is this koinonia with God and Christ, the Ekklesia exists.

We need pay no attention to the differences in creeds, institutions and rituals; but by loving Him *first,* and loving one another, we can be one in Christ.

All Scripture Bears Witness

Only this union with God in Christ can be the *center* of Christianity.

The Scriptures confirm this, as this fellowship is the theme of the whole Bible from Genesis to Revelation. Indeed, the relationship between the Father and the Son in eternity was undoubtedly just this fellowship.

John tells us, "In the beginning was the Word, and the Word was *with* God." This describes a state of being in the presence of a person, and is best expressed by "face to face with God." The *last* Adam was from the beginning "face to face" with God. So also the *first* Adam was created for the same position of fellowship,

27

and was "face to face" with God in the Garden until the fall.

God created man in His own image...why? God must have felt very lonely as he found not one among all the creatures with whom He was able to have fellowship. All the angels, animals, birds and fish were certainly very beautiful, but they could not come to God and talk and walk with Him in the Garden of Eden, face to face. Therefore, He created man in His own image—i.e., able to talk with Him, to meet with Him, and seek after Him.

To live with God and to have *fellowship* with Him was the sole object of our being created in the likeness of God.

This communion must ever be the center of the relationship between God and man. Without the existence of human beings, God could never be satisfied. God created man in His likeness. Man is a spiritual being, capable of responding to His love and having *koinonia* with Him.

God is Love! If there were no creature who could appreciate His love and respond in love, His creation would fail to reach its fullest consummation.

Even when Adam was driven out of paradise by God as a result of his fall—(fellowship broken by sin)—this judgment was not to destroy man but to ultimately save him from his fallen state and restore the fellowship.

One of the most strategic[1] verses in all Scripture is Leviticus 26:11, 12.

---

[1] See Exodus 25:8; 1 Kings 6:12,13.

The Lord said to Israel, "I will set My tabernacle *among* you. My soul shall not abhor you. And I will *walk* among you and be *your* God and ye shall be *My* people." This verse is quoted by the apostle Paul in 2 Corinthians 6:16 as referring to *the Body of Christ;* and by the apostle John in Revelation 21:3 as being finally, prophetically fulfilled in all the *fullness* of its rich meaning: the "New Jerusalem" prepared as a bride for her husband.

However, God was not satisfied to have fellowship with only those selected few. He wanted to be united in spiritual fellowship with *all* the people on earth.

Jesus made it possible to re-establish man's interrupted fellowship with his Creator. Thus, we have "boldness to enter into the *holiest*, by the *blood* of Jesus" (Heb. 10:19).

Fellowship between God and man, interrupted by the sin of the first Adam, was reopened! *Now* anyone can have direct koinonia with God and share His very life. Anyone can live a life of love and unity, *with Christ*.

This is really the center of Christianity, and "faith" is nothing other than the state of having this life-union with God.

To be justified by faith means God can enjoy this koinonia with *you*.

If we will experientially *practice* this living union with Christ, loving each other without any concern about sects and denominations, doctrines or forms, *then* we shall have the Body of Christ, with Him as Head. The

29

center of our faith will be restored. This is the Ekklesia in its truest and purest sense. Therefore, the Ekklesia is not an institution, not a system, not theology, not the words of the Bible, and not any ritual or ceremony.

The Ekklesia exists where there is this life-union with God through Christ.

5
Understanding Faith and True Unity

Faith *cannot be created or maintained by human efforts*. With the Spirit of God governing us directly, we love each other and do God's work by obeying Him. *Faith is but another name for fellowship, the koinonia with God.* No creed or doctrine, no priest or pastor, no institution or ceremony is actually necessary. The *one* thing required is that a man repent and come to Christ for the forgiveness of sins and the newness of divine life that Christ freely gives.

When the Lord walked on earth, He praised the "great faith" of a centurion and blamed the "little faith" of the disciples. He acknowledged the faith of a sinful woman, a leper, a woman suffering with a flow of blood, and a blind man by saying, "your faith has saved you."

In each case no doctrines, institutions or ceremonies were involved. Those who simply relied wholly on the Lord Himself were accepted, their sins forgiven, and thus they were saved.

The *only* condition was that they have *faith* in Christ personally—that they engage in a living contact with Him. Where there was this "faith," there was the beginning of the Ekklesia. Through koinonia they became one with Christ, and He became their Lord.

In a word, Christianity has its center in God Himself and in the fellowship men have with Him.

This fellowship of God with believers through the Spirit is the answer to the question of what faith is. It is also the answer to what the true Ekklesia is.

When this centrality of God in fellowship with men (through Christ) is made clear, we at once see that all other elements, such as an institutional church, the interpretations of the Bible, various doctrines, the morality of believers, or any other problem of different denominations or sects *cannot* be the center of Christianity.

This comes only by revelation. Very few who have been intently immersed in Bible schools and ministries will have this revelation. Everything that has been placed in their minds has solidified a mind-set. So many other things have been poured into their minds that it is virtually impossible to genuinely see the Lord Jesus as the one and only center and the only condition of our faith. To give up this solidified mind-set is too traumatic. It can even be physically and emotionally devastating. When this revelation dawns, we know that we should not judge others by any of our standards. Christ Himself *never* made these the standard for judging His followers.

The center of Christianity is fellowship with God.

The Bible itself is not the center. It is only the inspired *description* of this central truth, through which we may come to the center and have fellowship with Him. "You pore over the Scriptures for you imagine you will find eternal life *in them*. And it is they that give testimony to *Me*." (John 5:39). Oh, how important our fellowship with God is! This koinonia is the essence of the new *life* we have in Christ.

Redemption by the blood of Christ is, of course, the most important fact of Christianity, the basis of all koinonia with God.

To have access to God is the true purpose of redemption, while the propitiation by the blood of Christ is the *basis* on which we are allowed to come near to God. *Therefore*, the main purpose of God's sending His Son was to let us have this access, to enter into communion with God.

Only to *know* that He loved us is not enough. We must actually come into His presence and *experience* koinonia with God.

For you to acknowledge the doctrine of redemption is not necessarily experiencing the fellowship redemption allows. But all who have communion with God surely are also trusting Him who forgave our sins.

This relationship of experienced fellowship with Him is what God really wants of men, for this was the purpose in our creation. Merely to confess the doctrine of redemption is only to have found *the passage* through which to come near to God. Those who stop there have not yet come into life-union with Christ. You are in danger of dead orthodoxy! How full the churches are of this kind of "faith"!

Avoid making *doctrine* the center, rather than *life*. If I had been born in a country where so much dead orthodoxy prevailed, I might have been repelled by the doctrine of redemption, professed without a corresponding change in life and practice.

To confess faith in the resurrection is one thing; to have fellowship with the risen Lord is another. To believe in the doctrine of the second coming is one thing; to wait for Christ's return is another.

In all such doctrines, the koinonia with God is the ultimate objective expected, and all the various dogmas serve only as tributaries to this main stream.

Koinonia Versus Institutionalism

If you see (and some *will* see) that the center of Christianity is fellowship with God and that this fellowship is realized through Jesus Christ, then you will see the true causes of the divisions in the churches. You also will understand the way to get rid of them. The primary cause of these divisions is the institutionalism and organizationalism of churches *and* of missions. Instead of helping the life of the believers, they smother this life and fellowship. This gradually produces mere dead institutions. Such things can never produce the Ekklesia. Christians who really have life in Christ cannot exist within such a corpse. They usually will come out of it...eventually. If you do so, turn to Christ Himself as your center. Do not start the unnatural cycle again. Dogmas and creeds cannot bring Christian unity. Human minds are not so uniformly created that they can unite in a single dogma or creed.

Even our understanding of Christ Himself cannot be the basis of unity, because He is too big to be understood fully by any one person or group. Our limited understandings do not always coincide. One emphasizes this point about Christ, another that, and this again becomes the cause of division.

Only as you and I take our fellowship with Christ as the center of Christian faith will we all realize our oneness. There are different understandings of Christ. There are varying opinions about the Bible and its teachings. There are various kinds of institutions and ceremonies. But this need not hinder our practicing the unity of the Body of Christ. Is not our fellowship (however varied) with the same Lord? Is not the same Saviour our *one* Head?

Our fellowship with God in Christ is, as we have seen, the very purpose of God in creating man. In its fullness it is His "eternal purpose"—the ultimate—and He cannot rest until this is fulfilled.

I feel that all Christians are aware that this koinonia is very important, but obviously they have not realized that *this very fellowship*—not theology, doctrine, creed, institution, ceremony, etc.—is *the* center of Christian faith. When many Christians see this, the change will be amazing.

The ecumenical movement, which has become very

popular, seems to have arisen from the belief that the division of Christians into many sects and denominations has greatly weakened their power and made it almost impossible to fight against worldly forces. This is true, as far as it goes, but we must remember that the unity of Christians is not a matter of human effort or cooperation. *True unity must come solely from God. When there is true fellowship with God, unity will come naturally of itself.* The power of Christians does not come from human cooperation. It comes from life-union with God. It is the power of God working in men.

The One Body cannot be created by human collaboration. It exists by simply removing the barriers and having fellowship with God, a reality prevailing among those who obey Him and love each other. No other merely human method will avail. "Thou shalt love the Lord thy God with all thy heart, and with all thy soul, and with all they mind...Thou shalt love thy neighbor as thyself." This is the law and the prophets—and also the Gospel.

How Can We Tell?

If the center of Christian faith truly *is* fellowship with God and if only those who have this fellowship are Christians and those who lack it are not, then a serious and difficult problem is naturally raised: "How can we tell whether someone is a Christian or not?" Well, in the final analysis, we *can't* really know for sure whether another is a Christian or not.

For many centuries the distinction between believers

and unbelievers was made by their reception of baptism and the Lord's Supper. Yet, who can deny the inadequacy of these standards? Everyone knows there are many baptized non-Christians and many unbaptized Christians. The confession of creeds and doctrines is also a very inadequate criterion for recognizing Christians. These confessions can be made without the experience of the new birth.

Actually, we have created a problem that need not exist; for no final decision on a person's faith, or any standard to judge by, is needed for the simple fellowship among Christians.

Such drawing of man-made boundaries and distinctions is needed only for organizations and institutions. Once we lay aside the *necessity* of objective judgment, we *can,* in actual practice, though imperfectly, still tell whether one is a Christian or not. The most important basis for such recognition is, of course, that he confess Christ as his Lord. Also, there will be the reality of loving God and men in practical experience.

It is a lamentable fact that there is very little love among thousands who belong to the different churches and sects. This makes us doubt that these are really Christians, for "He that does not love does not know God; for God is love" (1 John 4:8). In the true experience of Ekklesia this will not be so.

I believe God is revealing to many Christians what the true center of the Christian faith is. The inevitable spiritual unity, which will surely result, will be one of the major steps toward the fulfillment of God's full purpose—His "eternal purpose." All Christians are *one* Body in Christ. We cannot create this. All we can do is recognize it. However, after we recognize it then we must *fearlessly* practice it! Disregarding our differences in doctrine, forms and interpretations of the Bible, we practice our oneness. We must receive one another on the ground of a mutual fellowship with God, in living union with Christ. This is the essence of the true Ekklesia. In such a free fellowship the truth will surely triumph.

On the contrary, if we put our emphasis on other matters, as has been the case in the churches since the Reformation, the great mistakes of the Roman and Protestant churches will only continue. Division upon division will overcome all efforts to perfect the Church. Certainly any attempt to form an *ecumenical* Church will prove to be in vain.

We must come back to this central point. In no other way can the oneness of the Body of Christ be practiced. I realize that to those who are used to the life of organizational churches, this principle seems very vague and impractical.

Put it to the test, and *really* live the life of fellowship with God. Practice fellowship with all Christians upon this basis. You will soon experience the reality of oneness. Those who have experienced a real measure of this *koinonia* with God *and* men...from apostolic times down to the present...those are the believers who *know* that it is the true, practical center of Christianity. Here alone is the pathway to the unity of Christians in the Ekklesia of Christ.

6

The Only Pathway to Unity

In the last chapter we saw that Christianity's center is spiritual fellowship (koinonia) with God through Christ. Where there is this *koinonia* there is the Body of Christ, the Ekklesia. Where it is lacking, there is no Ekklesia.

This is clearly confirmed in the Scriptures, this fellowship being the theme of the whole Bible from Genesis to Revelation. In *all* doctrines *koinonia* with God is the ultimate objective, the doctrines serving only as streamed tributaries to this river.

When there is true fellowship with God, true unity will come naturally, of itself—*if no man-made barriers are raised!* Therefore, we must receive one another simply on the ground of a mutual fellowship with God…in living union with Christ. This is the essence of the true Ekklesia. Here alone is the pathway to the unity of all Christians.

The Question of Doctrine

Doctrine was the very foundation of the Reformation. It is hard for the doctrine-oriented mind to consider unity apart from doctrinal agreement. The Scripture presents faith—not in doctrine, but faith in the *person* of the crucified and risen Christ. Such faith in the Lord Jesus is nothing but this kind of fellowship with Him: fellowship by the Spirit who indwells believers. This faith is not a conviction, but an *established relationship.*

The death of Jesus Christ was the essential basis for the forgiveness of sins, because "without the shedding of blood there is no forgiveness of sins" (Heb. 9:22). But the necessity of the death of Christ as ransom for our sins was the concern of God, *"to prove .. that He Himself is righteous and that He justified him who has faith in Jesus"* (Rom. 3:26).

Throughout Christian history men came to faith in the Saviour-God before He revealed fully how He would accomplish the salvation He offered. Abraham was justified by faith. Jesus granted many sinners forgiveness *before* He died. In these cases and many others, the atoning death of Christ was undoubtedly understood in the mind of God as the basis of forgiveness, but the people being saved were trusting the Redeemer *Himself.* They were doing so without knowing either the method or theory of redemption.

Faith is fellowship with God in Christ on the basis of blood-bought redemption. Neither faith nor salvation come by knowledge or acceptance of the doctrine.

It is true that only through the teaching of the death

of Christ as the great price of our redemption do we come to understand the immeasurable depth of God's love for us. The more you see His love, the more will be your conviction that your sins are forgiven. The greater also will be your love for God. The closer will be your fellowship with Him. Knowing God, who is Love, you will naturally express Him to others in terms of your experience of redemption.

The death of Christ is necessary for the forgiveness of sins, but our understanding of it is not necessarily a condition of salvation.

At the *last* judgment the Judge is not going to be so concerned about the doctrinal confession of those standing before Him. His interest will be in whether or not they have submitted to Christ. Jesus taught that many who are trusting their correct doctrinal statement (or their evangelical work) will find themselves utterly *disowned.*

"Not every one that saith unto me, Lord, Lord, shall enter into the kingdom of heaven. Many will say to me in that day, Lord, Lord, have we not prophesied in thy name? And in thy name have cast out devils? And in thy name done many wonderful *works? And then will I profess unto them, I never knew you; depart from me, ye that work iniquity."* (Matthew 7:21-23).

To the Judge of the living and the dead, theological understanding and doctrinal correctness will have *no* importance. *Heart obedience* will have revealed whether they really had faith in God. The Lord will judge men solely by what they *are* and *did, not* by what they knew and confessed...except as the confession reveals the heart.

41

Many trust Him without comprehending all He does in the work of salvation. Fellowship with God is possible for all who, repenting of their sins and submitting to His Lordship, will come to Him. This fellowship—koinonia—is the *object* sought. Redemption through the blood of Christ is the *means* of obtaining that koinonia.

If doctrine is taken as the center it becomes the cause of divisions. Doctrine makes one prone to judge another person's faith by one's own understanding.

God did not give His Son on the Cross to make the understanding of it a condition of salvation! The Lord Jesus shed His blood not to raise a barrier to fellowship with God, but to open the way to that fellowship.

If the *doctrine of redemption* should not be put at the center of the Christian faith, how much less all the other theological issues! It is not that these doctrines are unimportant, quite the contrary. It is a matter of *misuse*. If doctrines were not so misused, almost all the causes of division and sectarianism would be eliminated.

The organizational churches, with their doctrines and ceremonies, may be compared to a house and its ornaments. They are useful only if they help the activities of the Spirit in the Ekklesia. But the history of Christianity is full of examples which show that they generally hinder the work of God. They tend to choke the life of Christ with outward restrictions, hiding the true Ekklesia *and* her Head.

However, if we put fellowship with God in the center, these errors and these divisions can be avoided.

Israel and Jesus Christ

In the Old Testament God continually taught Israel that she should separate herself from the other nations because she was God's peculiar treasure. This seems to be the strictest kind of sectarianism. A misunderstanding of this exclusivism has had much influence on Christianity. It certainly did upon the Jews before us. But remember that Christ was decidedly against the spirit of pride that developed in Israel.

It is clear that Christ hated this sectarian spirit and national pride. The separation of Israel from other nations did *not* mean that they should boast themselves above others, but that they should come nearer to God. The purpose was that in their blessings—as an example—they might point all other nations to the one true and living God.

Jesus did not blame the Pharisees because they belonged to the sect of Pharisees but because of their *formalities* and *legalism*. He condemned them because they prided themselves on having all the truth of God exclusively. He did have a friendly talk with Nicodemus, with Simon and with other Pharisees. It was sectarianism that Jesus hated. The issue was whether they were faithful and sincere, not whether they belonged to the sect of the Pharisees. And so it is with us today.

Jesus warned His disciples against having this sectarian spirit. (Luke 9:49,50)

"Master, we saw a man casting out demons in your name, and we forbade him, because he does not follow

43

with *us*." But Jesus said to them, "Do not forbid him, for he that is not against you is for you."

John wanted the disciples to monopolize the truth among themselves. He wanted to exclude all those who did not belong to his group. This sectarianism, which Jesus condemned, is the spirit that dominated the Roman Church. That spirit was inherited by the Protestants.

Sectarians are those who would make fellowship with Christ their exclusive privilege. They are not satisfied with belonging to Jesus; they would make Jesus belong to them alone.

Jesus condemned the Pharisees because of their hypocrisy and lack of love. He wanted all men to come to Him and have koinonia with Him, but He did not intend that those who did come to Him should have any exclusive group around Him. He chose twelve disciples to preach the Kingdom of God, not to create a sect.

Nor did He flatter people who were in power, such as Nicodemus and Joseph of Arimathea. If He had compromised with the Pharisees, He could probably have obtained worldly influence. But He wanted to raise up followers to communicate *Life*. He wanted to build a kingdom *not of this world... nor according to its principles*.

Jesus had no thought of creating an organization or formal group around Himself, nor did He teach disciples to form any such organized group. Everything was dependent on the Spirit's uniting men to God through their faith. How different Jesus was from those sectarians who search sea and land to make a member of their group, only to make him twice as much the child of hell as themselves (Matt.23:25).

All that Christ wanted was for His followers to have faith in Himself. He had no interest in any institutional organization with worldly offices and laws. Neither did He give any dogmas or creeds which may be used to distinguish believers from non-believers. When He praised the faith of people, it was not because of their orthodox theology or the fact that they belonged to some organization, but on account of their simple faith in His person.

Simple faith in the person of Jesus Christ Himself, apart from *any* doctrinal instruction or theological understanding, is illustrated by the centurion of Capernaum, the woman having an issue of blood, one of the ten lepers of Samaria, the blind beggar of Jericho and the woman of Canaan.[1] Jesus wants us to have this same simple faith in Him. *This faith* with its resultant *life in the Spirit,* forms the vital link between God and man. Those with *this faith* constitute the Body of Christ.

---

[1] Luke 7:9; 8:48; 17:19; Matt.15:28

7

Paul, John and Peter

Paul had a very deep insight into the nature of the Ekklesia. He taught that Christ is the Head of the Ekklesia and we believers, being joined to Him as members, are therefore one Body—His Body.[1] When we believe, we are united to Christ by the Spirit. By faith alone are we joined to His Body. By "faith" Paul meant the same thing that Jesus meant—that is, wholehearted love for, and koinonia with, Christ. He made this clear by citing Abraham as the great example of faith. Yet, please note that Abraham had no "doctrine" of redemption when he was made righteous.

Without this *living* faith, this life-union with Jesus Christ, we are not Christians. Believe every Bible doctrine, be baptized a hundred times, join a magnificent institution that has world-wide renown, and you still do not have life-union with Jesus Christ.

---

[1] Ephesians 5:23; Col 1:18; 1 Cor. 12:1-31

Paul insisted that believers in Christ should be of one mind and live in harmony with one another.[2] He pointed out that just as the various members of the physical body are very different, the gifts and functions of Christians are so different that they may have some difficulty in believing that other members are united to the same Head and compose the same Body.

Thus Paul warns the ear not to say to the eye that it does not belong to the body, just because it is not like the ear. And likewise he warns the hand not to say to the foot that there is no need of it (1 Cor. 12:21). All the members with their different gifts and functions should act in harmony. Each is united to Christ the Head.

It is true that Paul was very quick to condemn any tampering with the fundamental points of the Gospel. Why? This was not because of technicalities or sectarian interests, but because the vital question of union with Christ was in danger. If, for example, someone questioned the resurrection of Christ, Paul rose to battle. Why? Because union with a dead man cannot create life. We live in Christ, because He lives in His resurrection life.

But in matters of secondary importance, Paul teaches us to be very tolerant with differences in opinion. He gives perfect freedom, hardly bothering to point out who he feels is right in a controversy.

Take for example the questions of whether one should eat only vegetables or everything, or whether or

―――

[2]Romans 12:16; 15:5,6; Phil. 2:2; 4:2; 2 Cor. 13:11.

48

not one day should be esteemed above the other (Rom. 14). He teaches that no one should pass judgment on another's (i.e. God's) servant, but should rather search his *own* heart and life, resolving never to put a stumbling block or hindrance in the way of a brother. Leaving each believer to settle with his God the unimportant matters which are his own personal responsibility, we should live in harmony with one another in the love of Christ and together, with one voice, glorify the God and Father of our Lord Jesus Christ (Rom. 14:5,6; 1 Cor. 1:10).

Paul is said to have been the first theologian of Christianity. In a certain sense, this is true; however, not in our modern sense of the word. He explained the Gospel clearly out of his experience and revelation. He always wrote to churches, not to anyone else. Even 1 Timothy, 2 Timothy, and Titus are letters to workers, *about* the churches. Paul never thought of establishing a system of dogma. He desired to lead sinners into fellowship with God, through Christ, and into all the image and likeness of Jesus. Thus, he tried to explain the great principles of God's grace in giving us His only-begotten Son.

The important thing is coming into union with God through Jesus Christ our Lord, not coming to understand (or profess) any of Paul's personal expressions of truth.

"The letter kills, but the Spirit gives life." Paul insisted, just as did the Lord Jesus,[3] that men who become slaves of the literal terms of the Bible are killed rather than given life. How much more lifeless they are when

---

[3] 2 Corinthians 3:6; John 6:63.

49

they are bound within the walls of institution, dogma and regulation.

John

In the case of John the point is even more clear.[4]

According to John, to believe is to be in Him. "I am *in* my Father, and ye *in* Me, and I *in* you" (14:20). "Do you not believe that I am *in* the Father and the Father *in* Me?" (14:10) By many such expressions John put great emphasis upon koinonia...the meeting with God and Christ.

John did not give us any system of doctrine. His writings are so different from Paul's way of teaching that one is often at a loss as to how he is going to develop his point. He seems always to be endeavoring simply to describe the "Life *of* God and *in* God"—to catch the Life as it is working.

Life in Christ is a continual experience of Christ. Life in Christ is not a theory or a dogma.

While I was compiling the *Greek-Japanese Concordance,* I found a very interesting fact about John's writings. The *noun* "faith" was to be found only four times in Revelation and once in 1 John. But John uses the *verb* "believe" abundantly. Literally used, it would sound like this: "He *faithed* in the Lord Jesus." In his Gospel, he uses it about three times as often as the other three Gospels do.

---

[4] **John** 1:12-18; 3:16-18; 8:12; 10:9; 14:6; 1 **John** 5:5.

50

Also, John never uses the word "pray" or "prayer" in his writings. ("Asking" is translated "pray" in A.V.). I do not think it was an accident that these words were not used. John saw "faith," not as a formal concept to be formulated into some theological dogma, but always *as a living and moving experience, an experience best expressed with a verb.* Notice then the meaning of the words in 1 John 5:1: "Everyone who *believes* that Jesus is the Christ is born of God..."

John was interested only in Christ, the *object* of faith, not in faith as a thing in itself. For John, the life of a Christian was a life *with* God *in* Christ. Prayer was talking *with* God. Prayer could never be done apart from *koinonia* with Jesus. Since koinonia is fellowship with God, the life of koinonia is itself a life of prayer.

To John, the believer shares the life of Christ as a living part of Christ Himself, just as a branch shares the life of the vine. This means, just as Paul taught, that Christ is the Head, and the Ekklesia is His Body; Christ is the vine, we are the branches.

In 1 John 1:3, John points out that *the life of fellowship with Christ and the Father* is a life of fellowship between one believer and another.

Only in the one who loves others does God abide (1 John 4:12, 16). He states firmly that only those who have the Son have life and that he who has this life lives in a relationship of love with other Christians (1 John 3:14).

Thus, it is indisputable that John, although he understood the true Ekklesia, never conceived of an institutional church (or a union of Christians) on any other grounds than *life*.

Peter

Peter does not say a great deal about the Ekklesia. However, a close reading of his epistles reveals the same principles we have seen in Paul's and John's writings. He exhorts believers to be holy in their lives—both as Christians and as fellow citizens of a heavenly *nation*— to be of one mind, having compassion and humility, and to love one another earnestly from the heart (1 Pet. 1:16, 22; 3:8). For Peter this was the basic principle of the unity of the Ekklesia—the *spiritual* house made of *living* stones of which Christ Himself was the cornerstone (1 Pet. 2:4-7). Peter had no idea of establishing a highly organized church. He certainly had no thought of starting an organization instead of an Ekklesia.

You will find this principle holds throughout all first century witness.

8
The Essential Nature
of the Ekklesia

The Ekklesia is the Body of Christ, and its Head is Christ Himself. This Body is a *spiritual organism*. The Head and the members are *actually* connected ... spiritually. Because of this connection there is true fellowship with Christ, each member loving Christ in heart, mind and spirit.

This fellowship is faith in its purest sense.

To have faith is to rely upon Christ, *the person,* with the whole heart. It is the koinonia, or communion, of the whole personality with God and Christ.

Where there is this fellowship there is the Ekklesia, because there is the real Body of Christ. Where there is not this fellowship, there is no Ekklesia, though there may be ritual and organization. Human activities and human devices cannot make the Ekklesia. It does not exist outside of this fellowship of Christians with Christ.

Distinguishing Christians

Fellowship with God and Christ cannot be seen with human eyes because it is a *spiritual* relationship. However, the reality of this relationship reveals itself in the life of the believer by his confession of faith in Jesus Christ, by his Christian love towards others, and by his obedience to God as demonstrated in his conduct. Also, when one is truly a Christian he is sensitive to this faith-fellowship that goes on in fellow Christians. This results in the growth of Christian bonding.

It is so obvious here in Japan that the churches are impatient to make baptized members, often trying to induce, sometimes even to compel, seekers of the Gospel to be baptized. The consequence of premature baptism is that many of them fall away, not even attending the church meetings, much less evidencing real faith.

The acceptance of creeds should not be taken as a proof of one's being a real Christian. There is a critical difference between the acceptance of creeds and fellowship with God. The former is a question of reason and knowledge, while the latter is a question of the Spirit giving *life*.

Serious confusion has resulted when churches have assumed attitudes proper only to the Head of the Body. We must always clearly distinguish between the churches of men and the Ekklesia of Christ—the Body in which He *lives*.

We have come to doubt that the spiritual relationship God has given us and the relationship we have with one another is sufficient as the basis of true and full fellow-

ship. This doubt exists because free fellowship has been so hindered and so hidden by the chains of institutionalism.

Let the life-giving power of the Spirit set you free from this false ecclesiasticism. We must be set free if we are ever to realize true Christian fellowship.

The new life that we are given is a *real* life and will express itself in *practical* living. Those who are having fellowship with the Lord will not find it difficult to locate fellow believers. All who are "looking to Jesus" will recognize each other. *This might be called an instinct of the new life*. The stronger the faith, the keener this sense. Those who are having the most vital fellowship with Christ in this new life can most easily identify those who have the same life!

Another important point to grasp is that in the light of the true Ekklesia *it is not necessary to place a doctrinal or geographic boundary on the Body of Christ*. Churches find it necessary to do this in order to carry out organizational activities and functions. The essence of the real Ekklesia—and the divine touch of koinonia—are there, though there may be no "church," as such.

When living a life of fellowship with the Lord, we will realize in practice the true fellowship of the Ekklesia with all other Christians. This is natural to believers. (That is, *if* all other elements, such as creeds, rituals, institutions and understandings of the Bible are *secondary*.) Fellowship with each other is entirely the result of fellowship with Christ. Thus, this koinonia with Him is truly our center.

When united on this simple basis, Christians will be tolerant of differences of opinion and practice. They will love each other with the love of Christ. In this love we see the hope of that oneness of all Christians for which we yearn.

"If anyone says, I love God, and hates his brother, he is a liar." (1 John 4:20) We can generally tell by the conduct and the attitude of a person's daily life whether his confession is sincere or not.

Moreover, those who really have fellowship with Christ cannot but propagate the Gospel. They will witness to their daily experience of Christ within the Ekklesia. Those to whom spiritual gifts are given, especially gifts of teaching or preaching, will be using this ability. In this way God will cause the Ekklesia to grow from faith to faith. That is, to grow in Christ, from one level of faith to a deeper level of faith.

9

What About Sects and Denominations?

If then it is true that the Ekklesia exists wherever there is fellowship with God in Christ and the consequent fellowship among believers, then what about the churches which are currently established? How should we react to all the creeds, dogmas, doctrines, interpretations of the Bible, ceremonies, sacraments and legal systems?

Variety Essential

In the first place, we should not seek to avoid variety in doctrinal and practical matters. Man is a creation of God; and God does not create like a factory, by mass production. Every person is individually created by God. He is an independent being. He is more or less different from all others. We err if we expect to find mechanical similarity among men, even among the children of God. The Ekklesia is *one* Body consisting of many independent, though inter-dependent, personalities. Even biological science tells us that the more life is developed the more complex its construction.

Some believers have deep theological insights, others passionate evangelistic tendencies, some this gift and some that gift. There are also differences in race and language, in degree of education, and in social customs.

Each of us has our own special duty to fulfill. These differences, however, ought not become the cause of divisions.

Why do we think that division is always the only alternative to uniformity or sameness?

The varieties of human beings show the intended manifold character of the Body of Christ. Each member should *retain* his distinctiveness, in order to serve the *whole* Ekklesia. In so doing he contributes to the fullness of Christ in His Body.

Our very differences profit the whole Body, but only if each would be humble enough to recognize the value of the others. Why make differences the basis of exclusivism and separation? It is harmful to nullify the differences. And it is still worse to try to unify them by political or ecclesiastical power.

Instead of condemning those whose understanding is different, we should thank God for what He has given to us in them. It is quite *natural* (fleshly) that these differences be the cause of divisions. But Christians must not yield to this worldliness. It is pride that despises others who are different. *Respect* different tendencies, in love for each other. This variety among Christians will contribute to the Body of Christ rather than hurt it.

It is the failure to respect such differences that has caused sects and denominations. Instead of appreciating how greatly we need the contribution which those who are different can make to our faith, we have made our own differences a rallying point. This is *substituting our special expression of Christianity as the center of faith and fellowship, instead of Christ.* As a result, what God meant to be a *blessing* to the life of the Body has become a curse. Natural differences in people are now dividing Christians into little groups, separating them from each other. Everywhere we see believers putting fellow believers out of their fellowship! *Christians* rejecting, condemning and despising those in whom Christ lives, *because of differences.* How awful (in God's eyes) is the sin of disobeying God's command to love *all* Christians.

Can we so lightly ignore the Apostle Paul's words?

> "I therefore beg you to lead a life worthy of
> the calling to which you have been called,
> with all lowliness and meekness, with
> patience, forbearing one another in love,
> eager to maintain the unity of the Spirit in
> the bond of peace."

Paul goes on to show that the basis of the attitude he describes is in the seven-fold unity that make us *one* in Christ.

"There is *one* Body and *one* Spirit, just as you were called to the *one* hope that belongs to your call, *one* Lord, *one* faith, *one* baptism, *one* God and Father of us all, who is above all and through all and in all" (Eph. 4: 1-6).

In the human body the eyes, mouth, nose, ears,

hands, feet and many other physical organs each work according to the purpose for which they were created. The one never intrudes into the sphere of the others' work. There is no belittling others' functions! Please note that each body part fulfills its "calling" according to the command of the head. The foot does not say, "Because I am not the head, I don't belong to the body"; nor does the ear say, "Because I am not the eye, I don't belong to the body." The eye should not despise the ear because it cannot see the beauty of nature; likewise, the ear should not condemn the eye because it cannot hear beautiful music. (Read 1 Cor. 12.) Also note, the body functions in perfect coordination, even though each receives its direction *directly* from the head.

Saying this, however, does not mean that the Christian can believe anything he likes, and that just any kind of faith will be Christian faith. No, there is one essential that we can never dispense with—the living fellowship with God and Christ. This is the center of Christian faith, without which no one really can be called a Christian.

Christ *Himself* is the object of our faith. We believe in Him *as a person*. We do not just believe in facts about Him. Whatever concepts you hold must find their source and focus in the One who is the object of our faith. He alone is that Rock from which flows the water of *life*. Without this *life* (the indwelling Spirit) we are none of His.

Unity in Diversity

A most helpful teaching on this theme is found in the

14th and 15th chapters of Romans. There Paul uses the example of differing opinions about food and days. He shows Christians that they should not despise one another. *Note that he does not advise them to find a happy medium between the contending opinions or to average the two extremes into a compromise.* On the contrary, he admonishes that everyone be fully convinced in his own mind. Paul declares that God is able to make *both,* differing believers, stand. After all, both are serving the Lord in obedience to their individual conviction of His will (cf. verse 4).

The weak in faith should not pass judgment on the strong, and the strong should not look down on the weak.

In this connection, it is totally unscriptural to define the will of God by means of taking a vote! God's will cannot be defined by the wishes of the majority. Each of us must find what is the will of God for himself. You must each do what you believe to be the will of God for your own life, and let all others meet their responsibility to do the same. The will of God may differ for each of us, but that does not matter.

He leads each of us uniquely. He puts us together according to His plan. *Individual* responsibility is necessary for doing the will of God. God's will differs in each person's life.

On the other hand, Paul tells us that we should live in harmony! "…being in full accord and of *one mind*" (Phil. 2:2). First, this means that we do actually have a close and daily relationship; we are not body parts scattered everywhere, each doing his own God-told-me-to-do-this will. Paul says to live in harmony with one another in accord with Christ Jesus, that together we may (as a people) glorify God with one voice.

How, then, are those who are "fully convinced in their own minds" of *different* convictions able to be like-minded and to glorify God with *one mouth and one mind?* Is it not obvious that this can be realized only if the one essential center, out from which our whole Christian experience flows is the love and oneness of spiritual fellowship with God in Christ?

This is unity. Unity in diversity and diversity in unity.

The true Ekklesia has neither uniformity nor conflicting differences, neither individualism nor collectivism. She is *one* living Body, with *diverse* members.

This is a strong admonition against the sectarian spirit of the churches. The God-given differences, which should contribute to the fullness of the one Body, have become the cause of division instead of unity. Each sect and denomination has its own institution and creeds. When there is a difference among the members of a church, some of them separate themselves from their fellow Christians and form their own institution and creed. Such an institution and creed clearly distinguishes that group from all the others and thus becomes the cause of division.

Only Basis for Division

This raises the question as to whether or not anyone

should ever be excluded from Christian fellowship. The answer is quite evidently yes. But we must be careful to notice the scriptural circumstances of such exclusion. According to Paul, such cases arise when someone in the Ekklesia commits *gross* sin. Paul instructed the believers to stop associating with any so-called brother if he was leading the life of a fornicator, a greedy grasper, an idolater, a slanderer, a drunkard or a robber—even to stop eating with such a person. If he proved incorrigible, he would have to be considered as an *un*believer (Matt. 18:15-17).

Such separation is not among Christians, but is rather the expulsion of those who cannot be accepted by Christians...in spite of what they profess. If we allow such sinful people to mingle with the members of the Body of Christ, the Ekklesia, it is as if you allow a malignant growth to remain in your physical body. The whole body *will* be corrupted.

There is a fundamental difference between immorality or Christ-denying doctrine; and both of these are different from the variations in doctrine or practice found among individual Christians who basically have Christ as the center of their faith. Christ-denying doctrine and immorality will corrupt and destroy the Body of Christ. Variations of doctrine, on the other hand, will make up the completeness of the body! Nonetheless, Christians probably excommunicate more people for divergence in doctrine than for immorality. The unrepentant immoral person or one who denies Christ ought to be rejected and driven out, while the believer who may view many things about the Christian faith in a totally different way than the rest of his group does must be accepted and treated as a God-given contribution to the fellowship.

This, of course, does not mean that *all* doctrinal differences ought to be accepted. Paul's message was that "Christ died for our sins in accordance with the Scriptures, that He was buried, that He was raised on the third day in accordance with the Scriptures, and that He appeared to Cephas, then to the twelve..." (1 Cor. 15:3-5).

Some "Christians" in Corinth insisted there was no resurrection of the dead. This presented a very serious problem to Paul because the center of faith was fellowship with a *living* Christ (He "who died for us and rose again from among the dead").

This difference, therefore, was not a question of theological opinion, but a denial of the essential basis of the Christian faith—i.e., the fellowship in the Spirit with the risen Jesus. If Jesus did not rise again, this fellowship with Him was only sheer fantasy, lacking reality, and "then our preaching is in vain, and your faith is in vain" (1 Cor. 15:14).

Paul could not be silent about this.

But make careful note of this: Even in this case, Paul was not thinking of excommunicating those people. Paul had no institution (or organization) from which they *could* be excluded. Being convinced that they had no living fellowship with God, he sought to *persuade* them about the fact of the resurrection. By this attitude Paul demonstrated what a Christian should do when confronted with those who disagree on central teachings of the Gospel. Rather than driving out at once those people who did not understand the resurrection, he wished to help them understand the true Gospel and come into living fellowship with the risen Christ. Note that agreement on how Christ will come back, the role of women in the church, tongues, the doctrine of the security of the believer, etc.... are *not center*.

The Issue Defined

In conclusion, we return again to our reaction to the existing sectarian churches.

It is true that these groups have their origins in those variations and differences. These differences must be recognized and appreciated for their needed contribution to the life and fellowship of the whole Body. However, we are forced to conclude that the organizations and institutions men have built on these differences have only hindered and interrupted the life of the true Ekklesia.

Even at their best, these movements do not add anything to the reality and practicality of the koinonia with God in Christ. The Spirit alone produces this in the Body of Christ. Believers who are outside of the sects and denominations will find no need of movements, denominations, creeds, or doctrines in order to have full and complete fellowship with God and men in the Ekklesia. As to those of you who are within denominations, though you need not give up your institutional organization, you certainly must face squarely the issue of obedience to God in the practical outworking of the unlimited fellowship He meant for all believers to have with one another as members of the whole Body of Christ.

10

Various Issues Clarified

Division is everywhere in Christendom. The sectarian spirit has paralyzed the experience of believers being one Body in Christ. Yet in the midst of all this—in the darkest moments since Christ—there have continued to be those who enjoy a living fellowship with God and with all others they fellowship with.

The grace of God and the presence of the Spirit have maintained a "peculiar people" which the New Testament calls the Ekklesia. This simple, living fellowship, or koinonia, was *replaced* by (not *produced* by) the organized church, which attempted to express spiritual life in credal and ceremonial form.

A careful study of this Ekklesia reveals certain basic truths. Let us summarize them.

The center of Christianity is fellowship with God through Jesus Christ. This relationship to God is simply the state of having personal faith in the Lord Jesus and being in experiential union with Christ. This is the spiritual life that the indwelling Spirit gives the true believer.

All who are truly in living relationship to God are joined to all others who have this relationship. This koinonia with other believers is called "the Ekklesia." This koinonia with God is based upon the common possession of the life-giving Spirit.

The Ekklesia, as the Body of Christ, is a living organism, composed of all who are in fellowship with Him. Institutions, organizations, creeds, doctrines and ceremonies are not essential to this fellowship. None of these serve to determine who is truly a member of the Body, nor can creeds tell us who is not a member of the one Body.

Each member has a contribution for the whole Body. The gifts of the one Spirit, as He works through individual believers, more or less differ from one another; yet all have the same fellowship in Christ.

The inherent unity of the Body of Christ must not be impaired or hindered by anything. Organization, doctrines and ceremonies, which some may use to express their life in Christ, *should never restrict this fellowship, or be made its center.* Differences in understanding and practice are normal, even healthy. They are not a reason for division (or pride) among Christians.

Now, in reaching the conclusion that fellowship with God in Christ is the true *center* of the Christian faith, we find that many problems are solved. For example, Christians will come *naturally* to live as one Ekklesia, in fellowship with God. This can never happen as long as we retain our present conception of the church.

Many so-called orthodox Christians, though they confess the best doctrines, act very unchristian. Others, who doctrinally are rather far from orthodoxy, often are more worthy to be called Christians in their way of life.

The former, though doctrinally correct, have missed the essence of Christianity, and their behavior reveals it. The latter, though perhaps somewhat confused, have pressed through to *life;* and the fruit of that koinonia with God is evident to all.

Another stone of stumbling to many is the seeming difference between the teaching of Paul and that of Christ. Jesus stressed doing, while Paul taught faith. However, when it becomes clear that the center and final essence of both their teachings is life-union between God and man, we see that the difference is a matter of *emphasis.*

Up until now it was believed that a militant defense of the orthodox doctrines was a sacred duty of Christians. (This places the emphasis upon the mind and knowledge rather than the heart and its reaction to the dealings of God's Spirit.) Now let us begin anew! Let us realize this past behavior to be misplaced zeal. Union and fellowship with God—the new *life* in Christ—must be defended and proclaimed. *Then,* and only then, is doctrine to flow naturally *from its true and proper source.*

History bears witness to what I am saying. If institutions, organization, creeds, rituals, etc. become the center of Christian faith, then either the life of the Christian ceases to be the life of Christ (as in Catholicism), or the Church is broken into many fragments (as in Protestantism).

When we see this simple truth, the "golden rule" (Matt. 22:37-39) is seen in its right light. Though no one has ever doubted that this law of love is the noblest teaching of Christianity, there have been many in Protestantism who, in their insistence that man is saved by faith alone have failed to recognize this as the basic expression of koinonia with God.

Sad to say, the ecumenical church movement is moving on the same mistaken road. It is good that they seek unity among Christians, but they would do better to emphasize toleration and love among all the sects and denominations and to make the institutional and organizational boundaries of these groups as loose as possible, instead of trying to create one super organization—the ecumenical church. This, at least, would put their movement on the right road and be a healthy start toward the full realization of the Body.

Another point of perplexity has been the importance of the writings of John in expressing the fundamental truth of the Ekklesia. As John's teachings were practical and experimental rather than logical, John's viewpoint did not find its rightful position in the theology of the Church. Instead, the epistles of Paul, because they were more theoretical and logical, were overemphasized by the institutional organization. The epistles of Paul become the principal source of theological disputes and

70

divisions. John's spiritual insights are largely overlooked or not understood.

The New Testament is only an extension and fulfill-ment of the Old in presenting koinonia with God as the central truth. Paul and John are one with Christ in teaching the same truth, only from different angles.

11

Romanism as the Origin of Sectarianism

The Roman Church blames the Protestants for division, saying we deserve it for the sin of leaving the real Church. This accusation seems justifiable at first, for while there has been little division in the Roman Church, Protestantism has suffered from endless division. However, the guilt actually lies with the accusers.

The Roman Church is the most complete and best-organized totalitarian regime in the sphere of religion. It is the *logical outcome of the concept that the Ekklesia is institutional in character.* For more than a thousand years the Roman Church held Christianity in Europe in its grip and, in cooperation with worldly powers, was able to exercise complete religious control over all Europe.

This unified control was exercised through dogmas, hierarchical organizations, and enforcing discipline. Note the three sides to this sectarian triangle: *consolidation of dogmas, hierarchical organization and the enforcement of discipline.*

To achieve *conformity* the Church used the severe punishment of excommunication. Individuals lost their privileges of citizenship and legal protection from the state. (They also lost membership in the Church and all hope of salvation.) After the reformation began, those who were against the dogmas, teachings, laws or institutions of the Roman Church were turned over to the civil government for execution as heretics.

This combination of ecclesiastical power and political power had a tremendous influence on European nations. History has not yet rectified the damage of that era. Men were so afraid of being branded heretics that few dared to even think of criticizing the doctrines of the Church. Hardly anyone had the courage to study prevailing doctrines from a questioning viewpoint. The Catholic teachings, organizations and hierarchical authority came to be thought inherently holy and above criticism. The people of Europe submitted to this ecclesiastical domination; thus, all more or less came to be the faithful defenders of the Roman Church.

Persecution of the opposition is an inevitable evil policy of all totalitarian systems. This is true in the East as well as in the West. During the two and one-half centuries of the Tokugawa regime in Japan (1623-1867) that government had absolute control over the entire country. When the Portuguese empire expanded and its Roman missionaries promised to become the enemy of the totalitarian Tokugawa government, Christianity was prohibited. All Christians were very severely persecuted and Christianity suffered almost total annihilation.

Now in order to have the Japanese people to approve

of this policy, the Japanese authorities spread abroad horrible, unfounded rumors about the Christian religion; rumors so abominable about the practices and teachings of Christianity that it would destroy the nation. Thus, the people in general, without knowing what Christianity was, believed it to be the most pernicious religion in the world and therefore *justified* the persecution of it by the government. This mental attitude has persisted even until the present day. Most Japanese try to keep away from Christianity and abhor the conversion of one of their family. The Japanese were educated to hate Christianity and to feel a patriotic responsibility to annihilate this dangerous faith.

This is an excellent illustration of what also happened among the European peoples under the domination of the Roman Church throughout the Middle Ages. When men are under the same social and religious conditions over a long period of time, they come to accept the existing order as the unchangeable truth. The Roman Church taught the people to hate heretics. They taught that good Catholics defended the integrity of the Church's teachings. The people believed this. It became their *duty* to do so. There was no toleration for heretics.

The reformers themselves were educated in this same atmosphere, so they also thought it necessary to defend the true faith and to be intolerant of any heretics. The only difference was that for the Protestants, Catholics were the heretics! True faith was now the evangelical faith. The Protestants, for the most part, lacked the power to persecute the Roman Church, so they only fought against it with logic, reason, doctrine, and creed.

Because they could not exterminate Catholicism, they had to be satisfied with merely separating themselves from the bondage of its authority.

However, the reformers did not stop with separation from Rome. Having broken free from its bondage, *they made their own institutional church*. Almost immediately there appeared differences of opinion among Protestants. Having learned well the lesson of sectarianism from the mother of that spirit, Protestants believed themselves to be the defenders of the true faith. Their only recourse to difference of opinion was separation. Therein started an endless principle of division.

This separation has been especially widespread where there is much individual liberty, as in England and the United States of America. In such countries, where religious freedom makes the development of differences easy, people who are very earnest in defending and propagating what they think to be the only truth have no qualms about separating themselves from others. Thank God they cannot persecute them!

In Germany and Scandinavia where political powers financially supported the Reformation movement, things did not go so far; but even there the spirit of excluding heretics persists. Naturally, ways of expressing an attitude vary with each generation. Because separation from other believers with whom we do not fully agree no longer involves actual physical persecution, separation is simply thought to be right.

Since the great reformation leaders themselves had intolerant spirits (even against the other Protestants) their followers could not be expected to do otherwise. The persecution of the Puritans by the Anglican Church, the resistance against the free church movement among the Lutherans, the intolerance of the New England Puritans against everyone, plus the many other divisions in Europe and America, all this has come from the spirit of sectarianism. Persecution and intolerance still live among Protestants.[1]

Look about you and see how the Body of Christ has been divided into innumerable sections. Even more lamentable is the spirit of pride in boasting about such separation. Men see division as proof of purity of faith. Yet this outlook actually disregards the *central* essence of true Christianity. Oh, beloved brothers and sisters in Christ, this sectarian spirit, which sees heresy in even small differences of theology, practice and institution, should never have been brought over from the Roman Church. It has no place in the fellowship of true Christians. Yes, such a spirit is inevitable in an institutional system such as Romanism since this is the *only* way to achieve unity in an institution. But the Spirit of God living in the Ekklesia makes sectarianism not only unnecessary but a *sin*.

May God grant each of us grace to rise above *man's* church and dare to realize the freedom and reality of the simple Ekklesia which Jesus of Nazareth founded.

---

[1] For a thorough historical study of this principle through the centuries since Christ, we recommend *The Torch of the Testimony* by John Kennedy. Christian Books Publishing House.

77

12

Is This Unity Possible?

The ecumenical church movement has become an important element in the Christian community of the present generation, but insofar as it tries to create unity through creeds, institutions and organizations, there is little hope of anything but failure. It is all too probable that this movement may create another new sect with new dogmas and institutions.

It is very difficult to unify the creeds (and institutions) of hundreds of denominations. Many of them have very special kinds of creeds and interpretations of the Bible, and they are so proud of them. It would be denominational suicide for them to abandon them.

If an attempt were made to find the largest common factor of the many creeds, the result would be simply, "We believe in one God." All other important creeds would have to be ignored. If the least common multiple of the creeds were found, the new creed that came out of that would have to contain several contradictory ideas, which would render the creed meaningless. Even "fellowship with Christ and God" could not work as the creed of such a conglomerate institution.

This koinonia has no unmistakable outward signs. But such signs must exist in order to fit into a creed. Koinonia is a reality—not to be included in doctrines or creeds or institutions or rituals, *but to be experienced.*

Take koinonia as the center of Christian faith, refusing to have any creeds or institutions, or else have no such central element. Our unity consists of *love.* We are united in that love which we have towards those whom we sense to be fellow Christians and whom we know by their confession of Christ and their daily life of faith and love.

This may seem very vague. To those who want outward signs as the proof of one's being a Christian, it is vague. Yet all who have this koinonia experience know that in the daily life of believers the love of God will make the unity real and practical.

Was it not true with that little group who believed in Jesus right after Pentecost? (Acts 2:43, 44) On *that* ground we can have one Ekklesia in love. There may be many differences in opinions, but *no* enmity.

At present there are all the sects and denominations standing side by side. Each thinks it is the only true Church or, at least, the most *correct* expression of it. Each believes it is his duty to convert others to his particular faith. They put labels on themselves, which shows how much they weight their creeds and trademarks. They condemn the goods of other dealers as of inferior quality. They admonish people not to buy another man's product. Thus, on the Christian market the different brands are competing with each other in their selling campaign, just like businesses in the world. Sometimes they may have joint campaigns against paganism, but finally they are not satisfied until each boasts of its own superiority over the other. The churches can never have true unity this way.

On the other hand, unity is quite possible if Christians simply live in fellowship with Christ and, at the same time, with one another. Accept the differences in doctrines as reasonable variations due to individual, personal distinctions. We can even respect differences. Realize that this variety will, in many cases, make the life of the Body of Christ more complete and abundant. In love, mutually we can help to make the Body of Christ grow.

Take this attitude and, in so doing, you will never be puffed up in your faith. You will be able to keep the admonition of Paul to the saints in Philippi.

"If there is any consolation in Christ, if any comfort of love, if any fellowship of the saints, if any affection and sympathy, fulfill my joy by being of the same mind, having the same love, being in full accord and of one mind. Do nothing through strife and vain glory, but in humility of mind esteem others better than yourselves. Let each of you not look on his own things, but every man also on the things of others." (Phil. 2:1-3)

The glorious unity of the Ekklesia can be realized only in this attitude of *love*—forbearing and tolerating each other, respecting the special contributions of others, and thus perfecting the Body of Christ. This is our hope.

We must abandon the attitude, "orthodoxy is *my*-doxy and heterodoxy is *thy*-doxy" and unite in loving fellowship with Christ.

Then, as Paul says, "Speaking the truth in love, we may grow up into Him in all things, which is the Head, even Christ: from whom the *whole* Body, joined and knit together *by every joint* with which it is supplied, according to the *working of every part in its measure,* causes the increase of the Body for the building up of itself in *love*" (Eph. 4:15-16. See also Col. 2:19).

Herein is the real unity of the Ekklesia, the Body of Christ. Since she is an *organism,* there is no human method of producing her. Life as an organism has its source in life and not in any organization. *As long as Christians think of themselves in the form of an institution, there can be no unity in Christ.* The churches in their present state can never be united, because their very existence is based on the principle of division in the attempt to limit fellowship and visibly distinguish faith.

The Ekklesia does not need uniting because its very existence is based on the fact of an already existing unity. That unity is the glorious unity that comes from all of us being *one Body in Christ.* That Body, by its very *life,* is in constant koinonia with the living Christ. The most important thing we need in order to return to Christian unity is to recognize this profoundly spiritual fact: We are already one! Oh, beloved fellow believers, see this simple and wonderful truth. Then dare to let go of everything else and *experience* it.

God grant it to be so!

May we encourage you to loan your copy to everyone you possibly can, and encourage others to read this book. We can render no greater service to the present need of the church.*

A TWO-BOOK SERIES

Let's Return to Christian Unity is the first in a two-book series on restoring unity to the body of Christ. The second book is entitled, *Church Unity--How to Get There*. This book is by Watchman Nee, Warren Litzman and Gene Edwards. Be sure to order this book and read it, along with *Let's Return to Christian Unity*. Having read these two books we urge you to respond by forever laying aside the barriers which have so long separated the redeemed.

---

*Publisher's note: In orders of lots of 100 or more, this publishing house will seek to make this book available to you as close to our cost as is possible... hoping this will encourage believers to pass this book out to the widest possible audience, for the widest possible good.

Order Form

Church Life
Revolution—
 The story of the first century church .... $ 7.95
Climb the Highest Mountain 8.95
When the Church was Young 7.95
Going to Church in the First Century 5.95
The Torch of the Testimony 8.95
Passing of the Torch 7.95
Let's Return to Christian Unity 7.95

The Deeper Christian Life
The Highest Life .... $ 8.95
The Secret to the Christian Life 8.95
Experiencing the Depths of Jesus Christ 7.95
Practicing His Presence 7.95
The Spiritual Guide 8.95
Final Steps in Christian Maturity 8.95
Spiritual Torrents 7.95
Guyon Speaks Again 8.95
The Seeking Heart 8.95

Brokenness
A Tale of Three Kings 7.95
The Prisoner in the Third Cell 7.95
The Inward Journey 8.95
Letters to a Devastated Christian 5.95
Crucified by Christians 8.95

Death and Consolation
Dear Lillian 5.95

Inspiration
The Divine Romance 8.95
The Birth 7.95
Turkeys and Eagles 7.95

Evangelism
You Can Witness with Confidence 7.95

Other Books by Jeanne Guyon
The Song of the Bride 9.95
Union with God 7.95
Genesis 9.95
The Way Out (Exodus) 9.95
Job 10.95

* * *

The SeedSowers
Christian Books Publishing House
P.O. Box 285
Sargent, GA 30275
(770) 254-9442